SPIRITUAL DISCERNMENT

*the context
and goal of
clearness committees*

Patricia Loring

Pendle Hill Pamphlet 305

About the Author

Patricia Loring has been released by Bethesda (MD) Friends Meeting for a ministry in nurture of the spiritual life. This ministry has included creating and leading adult religious education and spiritual development series for meetings and Friends groups; retreat ministry; workshops; spiritual guidance; and writing. A graduate of St. John's College in Annapolis and of Hartford Seminary, Pat also spent five terms at Pendle Hill and completed long term programs in Spiritual Guidance and Group Leadership at Shalem Institute in Washington.

This pamphlet had its origins when she began Shalem's Spiritual Guidance Program in 1986 and found some of their groups resembled Quaker clearness committees. Looking for what Friends had written on the clearness process, Pat found it focused primarily on the group's dynamics. She was told she would have to write something on the clearness process as spiritual discernment herself—as Quakers who feel a need are supposed to do. The support of Bethesda Friends has made it possible to undertake the task this year. It is hoped that this pamphlet will be useful in clarifying the spiritual context and dimensions of the clearness process.

Request for permission to quote or to translate should be addressed to Pendle Hill Publications, Wallingford, PA 19086-6099.

ISBN 0-87574-305-6

Library of Congress Catalog Card Number 92-62676

February 2004: 3,000

Divine Guidance and Spiritual Discernment.

Spiritual discernment lies at the heart of Quaker spirituality and practice. It's grounded in the central Quaker conviction of the availability to every person of the experience and guidance of God, immediate as well as mediated. Discernment is the faculty we use to distinguish the true movement of the Spirit to speak in meeting for worship from the wholly human urge to share, to instruct, or to straighten people out. It is the capacity we exercise in a centered meeting for worship for the conduct of business to sense the right course for the meeting to take in complex or difficult circumstances. It is the ability to see into people, situations, and possibilities to identify what is of God in them and what is of the numerous other sources in ourselves—and what may be both. It is that fallible, intuitive gift we use in attempting to discriminate the course to which we are personally led by God in a given situation, from our other impulses and from the generalized judgments of conscience.[1]

Discernment is a gift from God, not a personal achievement. The gift is not the result of training, technique, or analysis. Like other gifts of God, its origin is mysterious and gratuitous. It is given for the building of the community and of relationshipwith God rather than for self-fulfillment or self-aggrandizement. In some people this gift may be given or developed to an unusual degree. Part of the Quaker experience, however, has been that we all have been given some measure of the gift of discernment. In a life lived with other priorities, the gift may be left undeveloped. But as we grow and are faithful in the spiritual life we may well be given more.

There is a sense in which growth in the spiritual life comes precisely in faithful exercise of whatever capacity for discernment we are given. That is: as far as we are able, we practice an on-going intentional openness and prayerful attentiveness to intimations of divine presence and guidance, both inwardly and in outward life and relationships. Our awareness develops in the context of prayer, our communication with God—not only as we address God but as we learn to listen for God. The development of discernment is one dimension of a lifelong, on-going conversation with God, in which we learn to listen to a profound and subtle language and to let our lives speak, as earlier Friends have said.

As we grow in the life of the Spirit, our lives come increasingly under divine guidance. We trust increasingly that promptings and leadings of the Spirit will show us the way we are to go. Quaker spiritual life is felt to culminate in endeavoring to carry out the will of God or to live in attunement with God's will, rather than in an experience of God. As we grow in our willingness and God-given capacity to do that, we grow toward living a discerned life.

The expectation of divine guidance has been a part of Quakerism from the earliest period. Hearing and obeying was part of the earliest Quaker message to the world. Fox claimed the gift of discernment for himself early in his *Journal*.[2] His injunction to "Take heed ... of the promptings of Love and Truth in your hearts for those are the leadings of God" is among the quotations most frequently found on meeting house walls today. The ways in which Friends have sought to become sensitive and attuned to those promptings have varied over time and with circumstances.

The earliest period of Quakerism was marked by enormous assurance that the promptings of God would be self-evident to those who experienced them. Many early Quakers did not distinguish too finely between a motion of the Spirit and the most pressing or plausible impulse within themselves. In that, they were also not too different from some contemporary groups which are among us. This attitude rejects the possibility of discernment either on the ground that everything that comes from a person is of God or on the ground that it is beyond human capacity to distinguish what is and what is not of God. This attitude led some early Quakers to engage in bizarre or questionable behavior as being divinely guided.

The cruel punishments inflicted on James Nayler for his ride into Bristol—and the persecution that came upon Friends in their wake— gave the greatest impetus to Friends to reconsider whether all promptings of sincere people were to be regarded as divine guidance. If not, faithfulness required thinking through whether and how leadings might be authenticated. The discernment of whether the source of leadings was in divine guidance or in human need or willfulness was no longer an individual issue when the community suffered for the excesses of individuals.

Discernment: Tests of Leadings

Like the early church in this as in so many other ways, the Quaker movement drew together under persecution and began to define its boundaries. Quakers began to evolve rules of thumb for discerning leadings. They remained rough, experiential, and uncodified, just as Quaker beliefs remained unsystematized. Care was taken lest the movements of the Spirit be limited, constrained or falsified by inadequate human perception or articulation. What we might think of as tests were, in fact, expressions of what lent conviction to guidance, rather than forms applied mechanically.

As a result, there are no handy lists of tests of discernment in the writings of early Friends. Modern Friends (and friends of Friends), who have sought to summarize traditional testing of leadings, have searched the journals of earlier Quaker ministers who articulated the ground of their actions.[3] It is faithful to Quaker spirituality, as well as fruitful for the discerner, to leave the discussion of how Friends have felt confirmed in their leadings in some of its untidy diversity. Reflection on leadings in such a loose context may be evocative and profound. Comparing leadings to a check list could precipitate the discerner into a hasty, mechanical exercise, out of the Life.

The earliest group of signs available to Friends as they sought to test their leadings is the "fruits of the Spirit" listed in the fifth chapter of Paul's letter to the church in Galatia. In that chapter, Paul sketches the characteristics of people and churches living in the spirit of God—and of people and churches living in another spirit. The fruits of the Spirit have been translated as "love, joy, peace, patience, kindness, goodness, trustfulness, gentleness and self-control" (Galatians 5:23 NJB). If we accept these fruits as marks of a life authentically lived in the Spirit, their presence or absence in a person, a group or a situation can suggest the presence or absence of the spirit of God. They have been used that way in the wider church as well as by Quakers.

Some of the fruits indicated what has been called the moral purity of an action: its freedom from self-willed, self-serving or self-centered primary motivations. Among Friends the spiritual fruit, patience, was perhaps the central test of moral purity. With good reason, promptings serving primarily the individual's own will or ego-needs (serving the creature rather than the Creator, as early Friends would have said) are more apt to be pressing, impatient of restraint and evanescent. Promptings truly of divine origin are more likely to persist over time, despite outward checks. Where time is not of the essence, Friends are often encouraged to wait, sit with, or stay with leadings for a while to see whether they gain depth and definition, alter or fade.

Obviously self-control is a closely related indicator of moral purity. The word translated as trustfulness is also sometimes translated as faith or faithfulness. The cluster of meanings suggests the purity of an enduring reference of the events of life to God; suggests a person who has relinquished the willful effort to control outcomes and other people, to assume a more trustful posture in relation to the will and action of God.

Early Friends articulated another test of moral purity as "the cross." It derived from the idea that "living under the cross" entailed a cross to the individual's own willfulness. Interpreted mechanically, this led to the conviction that the more humiliating to the individual were the consequences, the more likely it was to be a true leading. "The cross" was consonant with authentic striving to be free of egocentricity and willfulness. As a test of authenticity, it was inadequate. Many things mortifying to a person don't constitute yielding to godliness. Humiliation may easily focus attention on one's self rather than on God. Patience proved a better touchstone for moral purity than "the cross."

Another rough grouping of fruits of the Spirit illuminates the quality of a leading by its results in community life. Quaker spiritual community has been rooted in that mystical experience of being united in the Love of God which can come in favored times of corporate "waiting on the Lord"—as well as by being woven together in the outward deeds of love. To experience unity in God's love bears fruit in love of neighbor. Unity and love are different faces of the same reality. Early Quaker exhortations to meetings were to "love one another," and to "be united."[4] Friends took Jesus' commandment to love one another (John 13:34; 15:12 & 17) and the statement that love for one another would be a sign that they were truly his disciples (John 13:35), not only as a serious call, but as an observable experience.

The fruits of the Spirit, kindness and gentleness, are dimensions of the first fruit, love. The three are deeply intertwined with life in spiritual community and have served as aids to discernment of leadings in community. In discernment, it has been traditionally asked whether an action would produce more or less love, greater or less unity, more or less joy. Love, joy and unity can be signs of grounding in the realm of the Spirit and the capacity to bear its fruit in deeds of love.

The community itself can become the test or touchstone for authenticating leadings. The experience of being united in Truth produces the expectation that the perceptions of a person truly under divine guidance in a particular situation will be consistent with the perceptions of others who also are—or have been—attuned to divine guidance. Truth is one, not several, and does not alter from person to person. So the perceptions of discerning people may be extremely helpful in helping a person to distinguish or discern the sources of her own perceptions and motivations.

Among Friends each person is the arbiter of her own sense of God's leading. Yet Friends have not been unaware that an interior spirituality without exterior checks carries risks. While affirming that there is that of God in every person, they have been well aware that there is that of a great many other things in every person as well—the "creaturely" tendencies to egocentricity and self-will are two. We also carry other voices within us from our formative experiences with parents, teachers, peers, and other mediators of the wider society. Long practice of meditation and prayer underscores that it's quite possible for even an experienced person to mistake one of these other voices for her Guide. Early on, quite discerning people submitted their leadings to others whose capacity for discernment they respected—usually informally by letter or a talk.

In discerning a formal leading in ministry to the body of Friends, it became customary to bring it into the corporate discernment process of the meeting for business. The assumptions underlying the process of the meeting for business in discerning leadings, are the same as those for its discernment of the rightness of any other action. The basis of discernment in a meeting for business is unity. The unity sought is NOT simple agreement, consensus, compromise or irreducible minimum of views. What is sought is a sense of that deep, interior unity which is a sign the members are consciously gathered together in God and may therefore trust their corporate guidance. **The experience known as the gathered meeting for worship is the basis of unity in the context of The meeting for worship for the conduct of business.**

The felt gathering in God tends to illuminate and clarify motives, to dissolve or harmonize differences—or allow them to stand side by side in the tenderness accompanying gathering in the spirit of God. Unity may enable a way forward to be found even if members continue to hold differing views. Divisiveness, disruption or simple lack of unity indicate that one, all or some members of the group are not fully under guidance. In any case, Friends have traditionally so valued the fruit of group discernment that they have been willing to labor hard and to wait long to come into unity with one another before proceeding in a matter of substance. Such unity is the Quaker touchstone, par excellence, of being guided by the Spirit of God.

Another way of testing the consistency of leadings against others' perceptions of divine guidance is by comparing them with the Bible or with the writings of spiritual leaders or saintly people from Quaker and other traditions. Again, underlying this practice is the experience that Truth is one and will not vary from time to time, although it may be articulated differently. Friends have been aware that particular passages, lifted out of context, may be used tendentiously to support a strongly held view. For that reason they have worked with passages they feel are in the spirit of the essence of the work rather than with exceptional passages. Such an exercise can be very clarifying, not only of one's guidance, but of its place in a tradition of God's guidance.

Peace has been regarded both as a fruit of the Spirit and as a sign of authenticity. Peace interpenetrates love as the harmony concomitant with the unity of a gathered meeting. It has also been a cherished witness to the world of how we live with one another when we live in the experience and guidance of God. On a personal level, the reconciliation of disparate parts of one's self or of one's experience in a new, sometimes unexpected direction or action can issue in a deep interior sense of peace. Quaker experience has been that living close to the Spirit has the effect of such harmonizing and reconciling both within and between persons.

Feeling at peace with a decision or an outcome, even if it is not what one sought or hoped for, even if it calls for considerable hardship or change, has been a frequent indication of rightness for Friends both in and out of the meeting for business. At this point, peace meshes with tests of moral purity.

Some of the most treasured Quaker vocabulary of discernment is related to peace. Friends say that they are easy or uneasy with a proposed course of action—that they are comfortable or uncomfortable with it, that it would give them peace, restore, or disturb their peace. Disturbance of a person's peace is a common accompaniment of a new task or burden being laid upon them, often long before the nature of the task becomes clear. Faithfully discharging the task leads to restoration of inner peace.

Closely related is that other cherished Quaker word "clear," as in "getting clear." In the earliest period, the word seems to have been used in the sense of having become free of some burden. Getting clear involved discharging one's responsibility to God by carrying out a leading. George Fox's words concerning the final meeting he attended are reported to be, "I'm glad I was here. Now I'm clear. I'm fully clear."[5] Today "clear" is used more often in the sense of coming to intellectual clarity about a leading. It is more apt to be used in discernment of the shape of a leading than in discerning when a leading has been fulfilled.

Being Led as Response to Outer Needs

Peace—or the lack of it—has been one important part of the Quaker experience of coming under guidance. Sometimes an event or situation in the wider community or world disturbs a person's peace in such a way that some action will be required to restore it. Sometimes what is required is simple and obvious. At other times a prolonged period of living with the disquiet is necessary before the particular response required of the particular individual becomes clear. The response may require a re-viewing of the person's entire life, direction, and background in an effort to see how it is being drawn toward or intersects with the source of the disquiet. Friends not uncommonly find themselves in discomfort for which there's no discernable resolution. Sometimes it yields in an unexpected way to the "sitting with" mentioned above.

Modern Friends have not responded to their differences from the mainstream by divorcing themselves from the world and from responsibility for it. To live deeply enmeshed in the wider society, yet at odds with its values and actions, can lead to nearly unbearable pain and confusion as to where one's responsibilities lie. For the person whose mystical sense of unity has extended to the whole of humanity or of creation the agony may be acute—especially in times of crisis. It is difficult neither to become benumbed by the staggering weight of pain that cries out for help in the world nor to retreat into the group to compensate for the pain of marginalization in the wider society. It may also be confusing that pain in itself is not necessarily a leading into action. It requires faithful discernment to ascertain whether a desperate situation has, in fact, been laid on someone personally. It requires even more discernment to discover whether the ministry called for from a particular individual in a particular instance requires prophetic speech, humble and hidden activities, bold and dramatic action, professional service or some novel and previously unimagined course. For modern Friends, the range of ministries extends well beyond the prophetic word of traditional Quaker vocal ministry.

Implicit here is the practical wisdom that we can't all take on everything. There is also a vision of divine order which does not require each of us to take on everything. There is a sense that in a world under gospel order, or divine guidance, each person's appointed tasks would fit together organically, moving toward God's unknowable goals for the universe. There is a sense that we are not responsible for the outcome. We ARE responsible for faithfully discerning and performing our own personal parts in the process, leaving the outcome to God.

That also leaves us free of the responsibility for trying to coerce others to do what we conceive to be their parts in the divine unfolding. The more deeply we come under guidance ourselves, the more we discover that staying faithful in both the intimate details of our daily lives and in the larger overall directions leaves little time, energy, and attention for trying to bring and keep others up to our mark. Increasingly we find ourselves given over more fully and deeply to those activities into which we have found ourselves led.

We can be more at peace with ourselves, more at peace with God's having the overall management of the world and its outcomes, more at peace with others. As we begin to grow in the awareness of the unique and particular ways God is and has been at work in our own lives, we may also become more respectful of the uniqueness, particularity and mystery of the ways in which God is working in the lives of others.

Peace which is neither apathy or avoidance has also been a sign for Friends that they are in compliance with God's will for them. In the journals of the Quaker ministers who were called on long journeys, one finds repeatedly that the moment of moving on from a particular labor, or of turning toward home, is the moment when the ministers finally felt they were at peace to do so. The reason may never have been clear. It is the experience which was trusted as a sign of divine approval or permission.[6]

There are, however, no rules in this matter of leadings and discernment. Leadings come from the mysterious depths of God, the indefinable, the unpredictable, whose ways are not our ways, who is clearly not running the universe like a business, an institution, a bureaucracy, a family, or anything else within our ken. And so it can happen that we are required to be precisely the kind of prophet of God who is appointed to disturb everyone's peace by demanding attention to some ignored situation. It is a matter for careful discernment to discover whether it is truly what we are called to do or whether it is a way of trying to make others responsible for solving problems that disturb our peace.

Being Led as Growing into our True Selves

Divine guidance does not always beckon in outward events or situations. Some of our leadings are promptings by inward impulses to growth or change. There can be times in our lives when an utterly logical course, which was previously satisfying, suddenly seems barren or false—or it may just close down, forcing us into painful re-examination of the way we are to go. We may be seized by a sudden conviction that it is time to break with our past and begin some particular new venture. Sometimes we are going along contentedly enough when a new possibility that requires serious consideration is presented to us. Those who know us may begin to name a new thing in us that needs to be honored. Or we may wake one morning to find that a slow process of which we've been only marginally aware has crystallized, with a host of implications. Friends' fundamental attunement to the upwellings of interior nudges and promptings implies its own view of inward change. Traditionally the process has been seen as a very particular, existential evolution of a life as the person responds to God. To review lives in light of Eternity fosters growing respect for the unpredictable timing, interconnections, and ramifications of events, for the manifold variations in human lives.

From this point of view, each of us is a unique part of the unfolding of the universe, with a unique constellation of gifts, to be exercised in the service of God, in ways possible for us to discern on an on-going basis. In many instances discernment of our gifts lies very close to discernment of our leadings—but not always. In keeping with God's mystery and unpredictability, it can happen that we are led into areas of weakness or disability. This may assist us in learning humility; may help us be clear that credit for successes does not belong to us personally; may uncover and develop unsuspected abilities; may be an exercise in obedience, or function in ways that never become clear.

Most of the time we are led to function in the areas of our gifts. Indeed, we're responsible for doing so. It can be difficult to distinguish this bit of spiritual wisdom from a functional approach. The two lie close; and the differences are often a matter of intentionality or priorities. When we talk about the identification and exercise of gifts as a matter of spiritual discernment and spiritual responsibility, we are talking of something analogous to, and sometimes overlapping with, the socio/economic definition of and use of gifts. This is the world view of the guidance counsellor who usually defines the gifts of young people in terms of the economic system or job market and attempts to find the appropriate place for them in the system.

The identification of spiritual gifts does not begin with a system. It begins with the vision of the unique giftedness of each person organically in service of a harmonious spiritual community. It springs from a vision of the creation as the ultimate spiritual community whose parts are integral and function together toward an unknowable divine end. Such visions include a broader range of gifts and work than those economically defined. They also carry a greater respect for the personality and work of each individual—and a greater responsibility for individuals to live into the fullness of their gifts and work. Such visions both allow and require individuals to grow and change with the unfolding of themselves rather than within the demands of the economic system.

The development of the individual's gifts is for the sake of the spiritual community and the purposes of God. But the good of the community and God's purposes are not identified with the prevailing socio/economic system. Needless to say, the practical implications are sometimes difficult to manage within a system which makes exclusive demands. Over and over, Friends have found themselves led into the prophetic stance which critiques prevailing systems, calling them to greater faithfulness to divine unfolding.

In addition, there is no single identity or leading which defines a person for a lifetime. Unprogrammed Quakerism does not look for one catastrophic change or conversion to bring a person into a correct legal relationship to God forever. Its vision has been one of slow and steady change, of unremitting faithfulness, more a matter of character than of forensics. Early Friends gave this process the name "perfection." Unfortunately its modern overtones are harsh demands, impossible efforts, and self-righteousness.

Talk of perfection usually makes modern Friends uneasy. To go deeply into the writings of early Friends, however, is to glimpse humility rather than self-righteousness, deep willingness to continue to change and be changed, willingness to seek and do and become whatever was required of them in love and confidence in God.

People in other parts of the Christian tradition, grappling with the same spiritual experience and reality, speak of the process as transformation, of growing into a more perfect image of God. In a memorable passage, Paul says, "And all of us, with our unveiled faces like mirrors reflecting the glory of the Lord, are being transformed into the image that we reflect in brighter and brighter glory; this is the working of the Lord who is the Spirit." (2 Corinthians 3:18. NJB) It was Moses, of course, who had to veil his face after his encounters with God, so that the glory he was reflecting would not overwhelm the people he spoke to. This is the expectation of transformation by the Spirit of God, not just of one or a few, but of all of us as we enter more intimately into relationship with God.

Perhaps the most helpful twentieth century parallel to the Quaker sense of the way in which we are "perfected" is the writing on true and false selves by Thomas Merton.[7] To the extent that the self is founded on or constructed of the labels, expectations, or directives of other people, Merton calls it a false self. Whatever configuration is imposed upon the self from without—by reason of social expectation; the demands of parents, teachers, mentors; the desire to please or to live up to some externally derived standard; the distortions of abusive, unjust, or violent circumstances—is a false self. The needs, defenses, and powerful demands of this externally derived self are also part of it. What we normally use to define our selves is the false self.

From the outset, Friends have been wary of the limitations and distortions of definitions and credal statements about God. Quaker emphasis on the actions of God in peoples' lives rather than on a list of attributes of God, reflects an experience of God which is more verb than noun, more relationship than knowledge. One of the ways in which we are an image of God is in also being image-less. In our own ineffability, we reflect the ineffability of God. Self-defining labels limit and distort the reality of our selves, much as definitions limit and distort the reality of God. To the extent that the self is conceptualized rather than the activity of the undistorted upwelling of Life in the individual, it is false.

The slow, steady growth in character, which early Friends called perfection, may be seen as a movement from false self to true self. When we grope our way in search of reality, past easy definitions and conceptions of ourselves, we are graciously freed from the distortions imposed by "the world." One by one we move beyond conceptions of our selves, just as we pass beyond metaphors, symbols, and conceptions of God on the way into unmediated, unknowing, intimate relationship with the Source of our being. This *via negativa* into ourselves overlaps part of the terrain we travel on the *via negativa* to God.[8]

At the same time, we become more open to and aware of the intimations—the pure breathings, Friends used to say—of the spirit in us. At the entry of that pure breath of Life into us, at its taking shape in us and our response, we find our most authentic self. In some sense we see the truth of our selves in the upwellings of that pure Light, Life, Power as it becomes shaped by the matrix of our uniqueness. We remain a self unique in all the creation, in intimate communication with the personalness of God. We draw closer to all the other selves, to the extent that all are living close to the Source, the Way, the Truth and the Life.

The effort to come to the true self and to be led through it, is discernment at its most profound level. To undertake to live a discerned life, to endeavor daily to be attuned to authentic movements of the Spirit leading us into greater fullness of life, is a strenuous undertaking. The spiritual responsibility to discern whether the source of our interior promptings is in our true or false self, to grasp the direction of changes and what they require of us, is especially weighty at the turning points of our lives. At those moments when the inner movement of our growth intersects the cry of need in the world, we require not only the disciplined practice of prayer, but the loving and discerning support of spiritual community as well.

The Role of the Community in Personal Discernment[9]

Quaker tradition held the expectation that God would raise up prophets within the community to speak to people for the good of the community and the world. The prophetic role was seen as a matter of community concern, entrusted to the individual. The individual and the community were accountable to each other for it. The gathered meeting for business had the authority to authenticate a person's concern. When the community sensed that a leading was "of God," it minuted its discernment. With that, the individual became accountable to the community which had embraced the leading as of God, to carry it out.

In turn, the community became accountable to the individual and to God to assist in whatever way was necessary to carry out the leading. In early times this usually meant help in kind, such as provision of horses or passage on ship, care of the minister's family during his absence, maintenance of a farm or business. It also meant the support of companions on his way. In more recent times, as economies have changed, it has sometimes meant overt financial assistance for the period of the ministry. There have been fewer people traveling or working under concern than formerly, partly because of alterations in economics; partly because of the erosion of the sense of mutual accountability between the individual and the meeting community; and partly because of an attenuation of the sense that leadings into the variety of ministries among modern, unprogrammed Friends are God-given.

To assist one another in the on-going discernment, we function in ways traditionally associated with the deepest work of spiritual communities. We can cultivate an environment among us which will foster one another's spiritual growth by directing and redirecting intention and attention to God; by discouraging what draws us away; by loving support for each other in the vicissitudes of our utterly human lives; by respecting and cherishing the uniqueness of each life. We may all be like gardeners who faithfully weed, water, and mulch. But the process of growth arises from the interaction of the mysterious powers of God and the equally mysterious responsiveness of the individual.

The responsibility for spiritual nurture is shared by the members of the meeting. Some may have a greater gift for it, just as others may have greater administrative, financial, teaching, or preaching gifts. While contemporary, unprogrammed Friends seem to be moving toward recognition of a greater variety of gifts, earlier Friends emphasized two major spiritual gifts for the nurture of the spiritual community. The most public was the gift of vocal ministry: inspired preaching whose goal was to bring the community beyond outward preaching to the inward Teacher and Guide, to direct people to the interior experience of the Life and Light.

Less visible was the elder whose gift, calling, and responsibility was the nurture of the spiritual community and particularly of vocal ministers. Of the range of ways in which eldership was exercised, we are looking primarily at elders as discerners. Part of their gift was the ability referred to by Paul as "the discernment of spirits" (1 Corinthians 12:10): to distinguish what was arising from God for building up the community—and what was arising from, or excessively mixed with, some other source.

In the case of vocal ministry, the elder's discernment might have been whether the words welled up from profound experience of Truth, for the community—or arose primarily from need to be noticed, to be thought wise or good or helpful, from the desire to press a personal view, or from some other need of the false self. The elder might help the needy to find some other way to care for their needs, while safe-guarding the ministry as a prophetic function for the spiritual guidance of the community. A further development of the gift might enable the elder to discern persons who were being divinely led into vocal ministry on a continuing basis. In full flower, the gift might include the ability to offer guidance and encouragement to people being led into ministry.

Earlier Friends emphasized the purity of spiritual intuition in guidance. Careful reading of journals and letters with modern psychological sophistication confirms that "pure" intuition was mixed with and grounded in personal experience of life. The elder's interior experience of God's work in his own heart and life was integrated with sensitively observed experience of life in Quaker community to shape his discernment and guidance of others, spirits. The image of the hollow reed through which the Spirit might blow has been replaced by more complex understandings of the ways in which the experiences of a life time can be gathered up, reinterpreted, and redirected by a leading of God.

The proportions of intuition and outward evidences in discernment varied depending on the individual elder. In the nineteenth century, the proportion shifted heavily in the direction of outward evidences. Rather than feeling one's way to an inner sense of whether someone was "in the Life" or whether the fruits of the Spirit were evident, elders increasingly accepted outward signs as authoritative evidence of the spiritual state. The potential quality of a particular partnership in marriage was not even examined if one member was from outside the Society or from another branch of the Society. Unity in the Spirit was judged by conformity to a code of dress. Commitment to God was brought into question by interest in the arts. Frivolity was ascertained by the length of bonnet strings. Freedom from the Law, to live in the Spirit, discovered by Paul, rediscovered by early Friends, was lost in a new legalism: discernment by outward rules.

Great numbers of Friends flouted the legalisms of nineteenth-century Quakerism and were disowned. Increasing numbers fell away, refusing the heavy hand of a misconceived discipline. This sad perversion of discernment by a people who professed to be guided by the spirit of God rather than by human rules was one major factor in the near-demise of unprogrammed Friends. Among the saving factors was the abolition of eldership as an office among all but Conservative, North American Friends. As often happens in such house-cleanings, most of the positive, nurturing dimensions of eldership were abolished along with the negative.

Some assure us that God continues to raise up among us people with the elder's gifts—that, in fact, no meeting would survive long without them. Today such people are frequently hampered by lack of understanding of the historical nature and legitimacy of their calling, as well as by lack of recognition, cooperation, and nurture of their own growth by their meetings. And, inevitably, others take authority upon themselves without a communal discernment of their gifts—from an all too human need to force their own legalisms upon the meeting.

The Evolution of the Clearness Committee In the Twentieth Century

In the early part of the twentieth century, there seems to have been mainly relief at the removal of the eldership authority. Friends welcomed a large measure of assimilation to the ways in which other people did things. Plain dress and language became less and less frequent. Styles and content in vocal ministry changed. More evangelically inspired approaches to social action were accepted. The "social gospel" had its effect. A measure of political action became acceptable and—in places—obligatory.

Young Friends became a creative force in the Society: finding new ways of maintaining the Peace Testimony and—in mid-century—initiating healing of the deep divisions and wounds which had separated branches of Friends for a hundred years. It was as if the spiritual gifts and power had passed to the young when the eldership ossified and finally disintegrated. Among some young Friends of North America, in the sixties, there is evidence that the lack of a structure for discerning gifts and leadings was missed sufficiently to evoke the characteristic creativity of that group. It is members of this body who began the current adaptation of clearness committees to discerning leadings and other questions of spiritual import in individual's lives.[10]

The clearness committee had been used by Friends from the earliest period to ascertain the appropriateness of a marriage "under the care of" a meeting. Such committees were closer to what have been called clearance committees or committees for the clearance of a piece of business to come before a meeting for business. The purpose was to go into the outward dimensions of the business or problem at hand, to determine what were the relevant and legitimate questions which might be raised in reference to it and to marshal information that might be required for deliberation. Discernment itself was left to the meeting gathered in worship for the conduct of business. In the case of marriage, the questions were as to the freedom of the parties from previous entanglements or commitments, their ability to live up to their commitment, etc. As with most leadings among the earliest generation of Friends, there appear to have been few questions as to the ability of the individuals to rightly discern their calling into the particular relationship.

Another traditional use of clearness committees among Friends has been for sounding requests for membership. Here, again, such committees have functioned more frequently as committees for clearance rather than for clearness, exploring possible impediments or legitimate questions that may arise when the matter comes before the meeting for business. As in the case of clearness for marriage, the applicant's own sense of leading to join Friends is often regarded as sufficient. As in marriage, the questions may shade over into those which probe the interior dimensions of the issue, blending with a process of discernment. In some meetings, such questions are routinely asked. In others they are avoided, in memory of the intrusiveness of the eldering system.

Among young Friends in the sixties, the clearness committee began evolving into an instrument for discernment in matters either too personal or not sufficiently seasoned to bring under the weight of the meeting for business. As Friends assimilated to the wider society with its high value on privatism and individualism, many issues formerly felt to be of concern to the meeting community have become regarded as private. In some ways this privacy is healthy.

In others, it severs the individual from the benefit of the group's guidance and support in times of decision.

As the clearness committee has been evolving, it seems to offer a way back into community support and guidance at critical times in peoples' lives. While functioning as an instrument for discernment, it also helps recover the communal dimension of the spiritual life in relationships, in the vitality and authority that come of profound union in and commitment to God. One mark of the clearness committee's vitality is that it has not been codified but continues to be flexible. Its flexibility lets it be adapted to a variety of uses and settings—and lets it continue to evolve.

Some members of Young Friends of North America were the link to The Movement for a New Society—a social action group formed on a Quaker basis in Philadelphia in the seventies. It evolved into a more secular group sharing many Quaker ethical and social concerns. Members of that group explored the use of clearness committees as a secular process in support of decision-making. Their experiences were outlined in a pamphlet with a wealth of observation and advice about the dynamics of clearness committees.[11] They have bequeathed us the name, focus person, for the one whose questions or leadings are the focus of the group. There was no conscious effort to use the clearness process for spiritual discernment although undoubtedly, on many occasions the secular search for a right decision and the spiritual search overlapped or merged.

The Clearness Committee as An Instrument for Discernment

While there are secular uses and forms for the clearness committee, I will deal with it as an instrument for spiritual discernment —and the consequences that use has for form and process. I'll speak of using the clearness committee particularly for the discernment of leadings into ministry, not confined to the tradition of vocal ministry or other forms of spiritual nurture of the meeting. In ministry I include our deeds of love in the arenas of justice, mercy, and peace in the wider world as well. Although use of the clearness committee is by no means confined to discernment of leadings, the centrality of acting under divine guidance in Quaker spirituality makes that a most likely use for the clearness committee. What is said in that context should be adaptable to other uses as well.

I will discuss considerations rather than offer a formula. This distinction is made in the spirit of the elders of Balby, with care not to lay upon readers a rule or form to walk by but as an encouragement to be guided by the Light.[12] As mentioned above, much of the vitality of the clearness committee lies in its improvisational quality, which leaves both its form and its participants open to the promptings of the Spirit.

If the object of a clearness committee is to assist with the discernment process, it's important that its members be people with a gift of discernment developed in their personal relationship with God. People whose own experience of concern has sensitized them to evidences of living concern in the words, behaviors, and lives of others are invaluable to the process. It's important not to just update the rigid legalism of the elder system, but to evolve openings for intuitive discernment. Depending on what is to be discerned, it may also be advisable that those selected have an additional area of experience or expertise that will help them see more deeply into where the questions might be.

It's also important that they be people capable of restraining the very human impulse to give advice, subordinating it to the discernment process of evoking rather than the authoritarian one of imposing. Some people also seek to have a balanced variety of personalities on the committee. Differences can assure that issues are probed from a variety of perspectives.

As the committee is engaged in a search for Truth, it is important that the group have the integrity not to feed back what they think the person wants to hear, from a misguided idea of being supportive. Support is given to the Truth of the focus person's leading by God and not to what could be a passing attachment or mistaken judgment. Discernment begins in a questioning, eliciting mode. It can be useful although it would be subversive of the process to include someone who is hostile. The more discerning the committee members, the more apt they are to sense where questions need to be asked, where pertinent background needs to be probed.

Parker Palmer, a friend of Friends who taught for many years at Pendle Hill, evolved a useful set of guidelines for the process. One guideline to help committee members discipline themselves to refrain from giving advice, is that committee members may not make statements or suggestions. They may only ask questions. And the questions may not be the loaded, stacked, or rhetorical questions which disguise much advice-giving. They must be

> authentic, challenging, open, loving questions so that the focus person can discover his or her own agenda without being burdened by the agendas of committee members. . . . it is crucial that the questions be asked not to satisfy the questioner's curiosity but to help the focus person clarify his or her inner truth. Caring, rather than paternalism or curiosity, is the rule for questioners.[13]

For many well-intentioned people, refraining from advice or commentary is an excruciatingly difficult discipline. For one thing, it violates the ordinary social use of verbal interchange as an occasion for display of oneself and assertion of one's ideas. For another, our culture equates helping people with giving them something: whether material aid, ideas, or a plan of action. If we haven't "given" something to the other person, we tend to feel we haven't really helped them.

The clearness process is profoundly counter-cultural in assuming that the greatest help we give is to refrain from problemsolving, to create a situation in which a person may discern for herself what is needed. Our somewhat shapeless, non-hierarchical Quaker forms arise—and receive what shape they have—from the conviction of the availability of Inward Guidance to each person. To enter deliberately into the discipline of restraint in the clearness process can be to reclaim the traditional restraint of speech at its deepest level, which is to wait on Guidance.

Whether the committee is discerning on behalf of the community or assisting the individual's discernment, the same respectfulness of the vision of the "focus person" is required. In neither case should the committee impose preconceptions or perceptions on that person. The committee's own discernment process may be subverted if members attempt to thrust their views on others. The focus person's discernment process may not only be thwarted, but she will undoubtedly feel violated rather than assisted by the imposition of someone else's sense of reality, in place of encountering reality for herself. What is being sought is the same delicately evolving, unified sense of underlying Truth or Reality as is sought in a truly prayerful meeting for business.

The Quaker way of trying to invite and be open to divine guidance is to begin with a time of silence. This is not the "moment of silence" which is a mere nod in passing to the divine. Nor is it a time for organizing one's thoughts. This is a time for what has been called recollection: for an intentional return to the Center, to give over one's own firm views, to place the outcome in the hands of God, to ask for a mind and heart as truly sensitive to and accepting of nuanced intimations of God's will as of overwhelming evidences of it. It is possible that someone designated or undesignated may offer vocal prayer for the joint undertaking. Spoken or not, it is understood that each person present will be holding the undertaking in the Light, in his own way.

The entire meeting is conducted in the same reverent spirit of prayerful listening. This disciplined listening is the counterpart of the disciplined speaking mentioned above. It is listening with as complete attentiveness as we can muster. If we are listening for the will of God, it behooves us to listen with our hearts, the marrow of our bones and our whole skin, as well as with our ears. Such listening is one dimension of the discipline of contemplative prayer. It is also at least as evocative as any question in drawing a speaker past self-definition and limitation, into the more spacious reality of God's will. Douglas Steere says, "To 'listen' another's soul into a condition of disclosure and discovery may be almost the greatest service that any human being ever performs for another."[14]

If what we are about is discerning the will of God in the life of a person, prayer and prayerful listening create the only conceivable context for it. It doesn't preclude laughter, a sense of the incongruous, the ridiculous or the unexpected, the possibility of celebration or joy. None of these has to interfere with the high seriousness of the undertaking.

Many clearness committees find a natural rhythm which includes a good deal of silence. There is periodic silence for recollection. There is also the comfortable silence that flows gracefully around questions and answers—when we give ourselves to really hearing them and considering them before responding. To truly enter into this attentive, prayerful listening is to let go of displaying our preparedness; our rapidity of thought, analysis or response; our intelligence or profundity. It is to allow the questions and the answers to sink into us in the silence which follows them; to sink into the questions and answers; to wait on whatever will arise from the depths, in confidence that—as in vocal ministry—when it is right and necessary, utterance will be given without our having fashioned and honed it in advance. We trust in the availability of God's guidance in ways that may be unexpected, even surprising.

Parker Palmer suggests that the questions-only rule can be relaxed about half an hour before the end of the session, to "allow the committee members to 'mirror back' what they have seen and heard." This does not imply a relaxation of restraint. It simply alters the mode in which it is being exercised. A mirror does not reflect itself or interpret what it sees. In my own experience, in the company of seasoned and detached discerners, less rigor is required in the nature of the utterance. One may trust the experienced intentionality of those present.

Sufficient time in silence at the end may allow a sense of what has emerged to begin to crystallize. Clearness may only begin to emerge at that time, however. In closing, it might be helpful to take stock inwardly of particular insights or promptings of the Spirit that have come in the course of the session; of the ways in which people were and were not faithful to the process; of the gifts that came of having searched with this particular group of people. A gift of tenderness and love is often a fruit of gathering together in intimacy and openness to wait upon God's guidance. It might provide satisfactory closure for each person present to speak briefly of the gifts of this time as they have experienced them.

Details of Preparation and organization

To be open and wait does not mean we come unprepared. As in the case of vocal ministry, we prepare, then let go of our preparation. We wait on what will sprout in the prepared ground. The focus person does quite a bit of preparation. It is important she first be clear about what she needs to discern. She also reviews in her mind everything that seems it might have a bearing on the question: relevant biographical information, any pertinent factual information, utterly un-factual intimations, longings, visions, dreams. Then she attempts to cull, order, and put into a FEW pages of writing what is most important for her committee to know at the outset. This will be a major step in discernment for her.

Her committee's preparation will be to read carefully, assimilate, and hold all the background in the Light; to seek guidance as to where the questions are, where the connections might be—without prejudging matters before meeting; trying to stay open to what is going to come forth unexpectedly and grace-fully in the process.

There are a number of other organizational questions which are best settled before embarking on the process: Is a discernment to be made on behalf of the meeting or is only the focus person to make a discernment? Who is to appoint the members of the committee? The focus person? The meeting's clerk? The clerk of worship and ministry or overseers, who have the care of spiritual concern, or a pastoral issue? In any case, it should be someone who might be expected to have a developed sense of the gifts needed for the work and of the potentialities of people in the meeting.

The preliminary decision of who names the committee members is a matter of some weight, with consequences for the functioning of the committee. Unfortunately neither meeting nor committee clerks may be universally assumed to understand what is involved. For the same reason, volunteers are to be discouraged. Many well-meaning people with a genuine desire to be helpful or a legitimate interest in the situation might have neither the requisite listening ear nor the capacity to restrain themselves from imposing their solutions on the situation. A discerner is required to name the discerners.

Where the matter is private, the committee may be outside the meeting structures and chosen by the focus person. Where the matter is of concern to the entire meeting, the process will be carried out within the meeting's structure. Overseers, for instance, may be requested to appoint a clearness committee. The committee will report back to overseers the conclusions of the focus person or of the committee depending on the situation. Overseers may report to the meeting for business, which may make its own discernment in the matter. There is a variety of other possibilities. It's important to be sure everyone involved is aware of and comfortable with where the lines of communication and accountability do and do not run.

With the weight of preparation and discernment falling on the focus person, it is helpful to have another member of the committee undertake responsibility for convening the committee, for the house-keeping details, for directing the flow of the process, keeping time and monitoring the quality of the interchange. Will this committee name its own convener or clerk or will a meeting committee or clerk? Who is being served by this committee? How is that expressed in its organizational details?

The route chosen should not be arbitrary but suitable to the particular occasion, to the potentialities of the meeting's clerks and membership, to the requirements of privacy and of legitimate community involvement. In an era in which the loss of community is being mourned, a clearness committee may be helpful in inviting greater involvement in one another's lives. We do need to be careful, however, that it not become an intrusion on privacy—or an exercise in attention-getting or self-dramatization.

The importance of confidentiality must be stressed. Conducting the clearness process outside the meeting structures may prevent the issue from becoming general information. For instance, if there were a question of greater openness about some previously concealed matter, it would be best for it to remain private unless or until there is clarity that the matter is to be made public. Even when the nature of the question is known from the meeting process, the particulars are confidential unless all those involved agree there is no reason for it. Even within the committee, the focus person may choose to establish areas of her life which are not open to questions, or questions she may answer inwardly but gently decline to answer orally. To enter upon the clearness process is not to abrogate all privacy.

Most meetings routinely enjoin confidentiality on their committees for oversight and for worship and ministry. Matters of weight, complexity, intimacy, or novelty may present an unusual temptation to talk of them with others. Everyone should be reminded at the outset that the clearness process flourishes best in an atmosphere of trust. Freedom to ask searching questions and to give honest, intimate, or profound answers—or to decline to give answers—must be uninhibited by worry about where they will be repeated or how they will be interpreted by outsiders—even spouses.

Is any record of the proceedings to be kept? Is it to give the focus person and/or the committee a basis for reflection after or between meetings? Is it to provide a record? Should it be a tape recording or verbatim record? Should it be a summary, a list of points covered, questions asked or the most apparently significant responses? Who should prepare it? How long will be allowed to prepare and distribute it? or should the entire matter be left as unrecorded as a meeting for worship, in confidence that the process will work in its own way and that what is forgotten is not required for the right discernment to be made?

The number of sessions required should be indicated at the outset. People being invited to participate may need to base their decision on just how much time they are being asked to devote. Most clearness committees meet for a single session. Where everyone is well prepared and gives themselves prayerfully to the process, the critical insights often emerge either within the session or in the subsequent weeks during which the experience percolates through the consciousness, the unconsciousness and back again.

Sometimes, however, the result of the percolation is that a new layer of questions has emerged and needs to be addressed in another session. This is ideally done with the same committee as previously—unless one of the revelations is the need for a particular qualification. It works best if the composition of the committee is altered as little as possible. In the interest of keeping the same committee throughout a longer clearness process, it's wise to reflect at the outset on whether the process is likely to unfold in stages or to require two or more meetings.

The length of sessions is also best mentioned at this point. Again, some flexibility and consideration for the particulars of the situation and those involved should be shown. Two hours generally seems to be the maximum time that people can function with alertness in this kind of intensely focussed way. Parker Palmer suggests three hours with a break in the middle.

In Conclusion

As a structure to facilitate discernment of the will of God, the clearness committee partakes of many of the features of a meeting for worship for the conduct of business. Where meetings for business have been assimilated to more secular models, with emphasis on getting through agendas within time constraints, on decision-making rather than discernment, consensus rather than unity, it is helpful to incorporate in the model some aspects of worship sharing.

The crucial element is the establishment of a context of prayerful attentiveness, not just for the beginning and end of the time together but for the entire meeting. Liberal amounts of silence between utterances permits them to be heard with all their resonances and taken below the surface mind. The space between can remove the temptation to revert to discussion or conversation. It can help reinforce disciplined speaking and listening. It can allow what does come forth to arise spontaneously from the Center.

If the committee members are trusting of the promptings of the Spirit and willing to wait on them, little structure is required. Parker Palmer's succinct and sensitive distillation of the clearness process fits on three single-spaced pages. It is tempting to prepare check-lists of things to look for: indications of motivations, of gifts unfolding, of where the true self has been developing, where the false self is deflecting it. Probably it's best that awareness of all these elements just be part of the preparation to be done then let go of, the better to see what is in the present without preconception under the guidance of the Spirit.

The clearness committee is another application of the Conservative Quaker dictum, "Prepare the minister, not the ministry." The situation is analogous to the meeting for worship where we go, purposing neither to speak or not to speak, but with a heart and mind prepared by a week and a life of meditative reading, reflection, prayer and faithfulness, to wait expectantly on what God brings forth. So we go to a clearness committee with heart and mind prepared, setting aside our own purposes, in holy expectancy of whatever new thing God is bringing about. As we wait, centered in silence, we trust we will be given the ears to hear what is significant and the words to evoke what is meant to come forth.

NOTES

1. See articles on discernment from a Quaker point of view in: *Friends Consultation on Discernment*. (Richmond, Indiana: Quaker Hill, 1985).

   The following non-Quaker books are also helpful in understanding discernment, although their understanding is shaped by other traditions:

   Suzanne G.Farnham et. al., *Listening Hearts: Discerning Call in Community* (Morehouse Publishing, 1991).

   Thomas H. Green, *Weeds Among the Wheat. Discernment: Where Prayer and Action Meet* (Notre Dame, Indiana: Ave Maria Press, 1984).

2. John L. Nickalls, ed., *The Journal of George Fox* (London: The Religious Society of Friends, 1975), pp 14-15 on discernment.

3. Howard H. Brinton, *The Quaker Doctrine of Inward Peace,* PHP #44 (Wallingford, Pennsylvania: Pendle Hill Publications, 1948).

   Michael J. Sheeran. *Beyond Majority Rule.* (Philadelphia: Philadelphia Yearly Meeting, 1983), pp 22-30.

   Paul Lacy. *Leading and Being Led,* PHP #264. (Wallingford, Pennsylvania: 1985), pp 15-23.

4. Hugh Barbour, *Margaret Fell Speaking,* PHP #206. (Wallingford, Pennsylvania: Pendle Hill Publications 1976), pp. 24-25, "Living Under the Light: An Epistle to Convinced Friends."

5. Nickalls, ed., *Journal,* p. 752.

6. Phillips P. Moulton, ed., *The Journal and Major Essays of John Woolman* (Richmond, Indiana: Friends United Press, 1989), p. 96, p. 135, *et passim.* Woolman's *Journal* is the best record I know of a discerned life, lived under guidance, full of examples of discernment.

7. Merton's thought is found throughout his prolific writings. For a coherent and beautifully written exposition see:

   James Finley, *Merton's Palace of Nowhere: A Search for God through Awareness of the True Self,* (Notre Dame: Ave Maria Press, 1978).

8. For a lucid discussion of the *via negativa* (also known as the apophatic tradition) see: Sandra Cronk, *Dark Night Journey,* (Wallingford, Pennsylvania: Pendle Hill Publications, 1991), esp. ch. 2.

9. The offices of elder and minister and their relationship with the community are discussed in:

Friends Consultation on Eldering, (Richmond, Indiana: Quaker Hill, 1982), see Samuel Caldwell on the nurturing aspects.

Sandra Cronk, *Gospel Order,* PHP #297 (Wallingford, Pennsylvania: Pendle Hill Publications, 1991).

Samuel Bownas, *A Description of the Qualifications Necessary to A Gospel Minister* (Philadelphia: Pendle Hill & Tract. Assn. of Friends, 1989) esp. the introduction by William Taber.

Alastair Heron, *Gifts and Ministries* (London: Quaker Home Service, 1987).

10. This development in YFNA, overlapping with The New Swarthmore Community in upstate New York and elsewhwere, and the links of both with the Movement for a New Society is still oral history, available anecdotally from those who lived it.

11. Peter Woodrow, *Clearness,* (Philadelphia: New Society Publishers, 1976).

12. Postscript to an epistle to 'the brethren in the north' issued by a meeting of elders at Balby, 1656, London Yearly Meeting, Christian faith and practice in the experience of the Society of Friends. np., quoted in "To the reader."

13. Parker Palmer, "The Clearness Committee: A Way of Discernment," *Weavings* (July/August 1988), pp. 37-40.

See also: Jan Hoffman, "Clearness Committees and their Use in Personal Discernment," twelfth month press, 1991, tract.

14. Douglas Steere, "On Listening to Another, Part Ill." *Gleanings* (Nashville: The Upper Room, 1986), p. 83.